A Minstrel's
Musings

SARAH ASHWOOD

Published by
Diminuendo Press
Imprint of Cyberwizard Productions
1205 N. Saginaw Boulevard #D
PMB 224
Saginaw, Texas 76179

A Minstrel's Musings
Edited by Crystalwizard

Cover Artist: Melvin Barnette

Interior Illustrations: A. R. Stone

Copyright © 2009 Cyberwizard Productions
Individual poems copyright © 2009 Sarah Ashwood
ISBN: 978-0-9821352-9-7

Library of Congress Control Number: 2009902045

First Edition

Table of Contents

For Carol and Hannah
Who willingly read everything I ever wrote

For Professor Lutz
The catalyst for my writing career

For my family, friends, and church
Because they are mine

And for John IV, Bob Tom, and Junior
Beloved by their Auntie Sarah

Forward

As Zora Neale Hurston said in her famous novel, *Their Eyes Were Watching God*, "There are years that ask questions and years that answer." Six years ago, I decided I wanted to be a writer. Naturally, the questions then followed, "Am I good enough? Can I do this? Do I have what it takes? Am I willing to work hard for it?" Now, slowly, I hope these questions are being answered in a positive way.

Six years ago, I never dreamed my first published book would be a volume of poetry. So much has gone into the writing of this chapbook that I scarcely know where to begin. When one says "Thank you" to those who have encouraged, guided, inspired, and taught them along the way, how do they say it? How do they say it *all*? I think it is impossible. Nevertheless, here are a few thoughts on the topics of thankfulness, writing, and poetry.

I have an abiding love of fairytales, a deep interest in mythology, and people like J.R.R. Tolkien, Robert Jordan, my sister Hannah, my brother Joshua, my cousin Carol, and my friends Calvin and Jesse to thank for making me believe of the fantasy genre, "Hey, I like this…and I can write it, too!"

I have Professor Michelle Lutz, from Northwestern Bible College in MN, to thank for recognizing, if not potential, then love and purpose. Not only did she encourage a young college student's dreams, she also advised me, in the interests of starting a writing career, to switch schools and pursue a degree in writing…something which, on my own, I would never have done due to the extra years of school. I have my college professors and fellow students to thank who, since that time, have praised my writing, supported my dreams, and challenged my thought processes. I have my parents, who homeschooled my five siblings and me, to thank for my first *real* start: teaching me to read and write.

I have faithful readers like Carol, Hannah, Susan,

Christa, Bethany (Rusty), Pa-Pa, Bryan, Mel, Towbel, and my friends on www.fantasy-writers.org (FWO) to thank for their advice, their suggestions, their compliments, their comments, their critiquing, and their refining of my skills. So many have believed in me from the beginning: Millie, Kayla, Joe, and Christina are just a few.

I have my editor, Kelly, to thank for first soliciting my poetry for *Flashing Swords Press*, then for the volume you hold in your hands. I have also Mel and Anne to thank for their impressive artwork. This chapbook, both inside and out, would not be the same without it.

Long before a lovely spring day in March 2007 when a long walk in our own woods would inspire my first real poem (*Sun Slayer*, which you will find in these pages); long before I ever dreamed of calling myself a poet, my mother and grandmother used to read poetry to me. Long before I liked poetry, they loved it, as did my younger sister, Mercy. I remember growing up parroting the popular line among many children— "I hate poetry." But even as I said it, I knew it wasn't entirely true. I liked the silly poems my grandmother would write for her grandchildren. I loved it when she would read aloud *The Highwayman*—still my favorite poem. Furthermore, I loved hearing my mom read such works as *The Skeleton in Armor, Stopping By Woods on a Snowy Evening,* and *The Raven*. I even enjoyed goofy children's poetry: Dr. Seuss was always a favorite. Mercy had a book of well-loved poetry, and she used to share favorites with me: to this day I remember *The Kiss*, and *My Love is Like a Red, Red Rose*. And then there was the first poem I ever memorized, *The Owl and the Pussycat*, learned from reading my sisters' and my picture book over and over again as a child…

In all truth, it wasn't poetry that I hated. It was the stuff that makes no sense and jars rather than soothes the ear, but is still considered (for whatever reason) "great poetry." This is what I disdained. Years later, I am still not a fan of this type of poetry, yet my horizons are broadened everyday. Perhaps someday I shall love all poetry equally. Perhaps.

However, for years, I not only parroted the line, "I hate poetry," there was another quote of which I was fond: "If it doesn't rhyme, it's not poetry." Now, I will be the first to admit that I *prefer* poetry that rhymes, but after years of reading and studying and being challenged by other poetry fans (such as TommyG from FWO, to whom you will find a poem dedicated that was written because of a private challenge he issued me), I have finally arrived at the place where I can appreciate, read, and write—with pleasure—poetry that does not rhyme. If any of my readers feel as I once did concerning non-rhyming poetry and poetry in general, I hope this book will inspire you to rethink your ideas and open your mind to the different forms of beauty out there.

In this volume, *A Minstrel's Musings*, you will find a variety of poems spanning many different topics. As a writer and a reader, I am very eclectic. I enjoy most genres, though fantasy and historical fiction are some definite favorites. In *A Minstrel's Musings*, you will find several poems devoted to both of these.

In the past, I have been asked what inspires me to write the poems I do. The answer is simple: everything and nothing. Most of the time, poetry comes easily to me. In *A Minstrel's Musings*, there are poems where I simply sat down and thought, "I need to write a poem." Once the topic came to mind, the poem followed swiftly. (Mind you, there was usually heavy editing afterward!) Some pieces in this book reflect my own life experiences, as well as my personal thoughts, desires, dreams, hopes, and beliefs. At the same time, there are a number of first-person poems that have little or nothing to do with me, except as their creator. That is the beauty of being a writer: you can become anyone and anything, and all with the stroke of a pen or the press of a key.

There are poems in this volume inspired by or written for special people in my life. *Life* is a gift for Lydia on fantasy-writers, because she's more of an inspiration than she will ever know. *A Strong Kind of Love* is self-explanatory: it is my feeble attempt to put down on paper the deep love I feel for my two younger sisters, Mercy and Hannah. It is a celebration of sisterly love all over the world. *A Winter Walk* strives, but doubtless fails, to capture the enchanted, ethereal beauty of a December walk down a frozen country road, beneath a fat, full Oklahoma moon. *Escape* reflects my desire to journey far away; perhaps some day I will personally visit some of the places I wrote about, but others I am likely to experience only in my dreams or in the pages of a novel. Then there are those pieces inspired by a simple, real-life event: I stepped outside on our front porch one day to put on my tennis shoes (trying to avid tracking dirt indoors) and up came my black kitten, Captain Stevens, purring as he rubbed against my ankles. Thus *The Spell-Breaker*—one of my favorite poems in this volume—was born. *Dragonkind* is my tribute to the dragons among us; and for me, those particularly found on my online writer's group, FWO. *Simple Pleasures* incorporates a number of life's little pleasures: if I could have named every aunt, uncle, cousin, niece, nephew, sibling, grandparent, and relative by name I would have, but this poem must cover them all instead.

Doubtless, it would take me hours and much space to explain the thought processes behind each poem. At any rate, I don't think such a feat is necessary. Most of these poems speak for themselves. It is my hope that as you peruse these pages you will find something with which you can indentify. Something to make you smile, make you laugh, make you cry, make you nod your head, make you think, make you feel, make you say, "I can understand that." Or, "I believe that." Or, "Yes, that's true." Or, "This is me."

If so, I have succeeded as a writer, as a poet.

Welcome to *A Minstrel's Musings*, to my world, and I thank you for electing to take this journey with me.

Sarah D.C. Ashwood, September 2008 A.D.

I write because I want to have more than one life.

--Anne Tyler

Introduction

I tried my hand at making dye once during the doldrums of creativity when the muse was obstinate and silent. I knew the color I wanted, knew the formula and all the technical aspects of creating it. In my eagerness to bring to life my vision exactly as I saw it in my mind, I made the concoction too complicated; throwing in too many allusive and rare colors as an attempt to make my creation shine. While each color was beautiful in itself, ttogether they only succeeded in muddying my hue. In the end what I lovingly, obsessively and loyally constructed was... a mess.

Poets tend to fall into this trap as well. Even those, or perhaps especially those like myself, who attempt to adhere to the "One word to encompass the thought" philosophy. We add not only the most complex terms to our creation but the most rare and obscure phrasing. We forget that saying exactly what we mean has an innate beauty all its own. That directness has a power. That the ground being of poetry is the physical being meant to connect with it.

Sarah is not one who has forgotten those roots. She has captured her images with straightforward snares that disarm and enchant. There's a real human quality that attracts our hearts to her words. Her subjects speak to humanity with themes of family, love and life (sometimes the dreaming life and the fantastic realms we yearn for) surrounding each with a graceful but intense innocence, obvious understanding few can capture.

Natural has a subtle rhythmic force that drives the poem with a constant pull. *Lady* is rich and supple with vivid imagery, the duality of which is inveiglingly powerful. *Simple Pleasures* connected me to the memories of family I had thought forgotten, a very rare feat. *Dance of War* reads as a narrative in construct with its movement and energy. And *Binding Curse* revisits the powerful and mystical in a very human way while echoing with that lost art of the Epic Poem; as so many of hers do.

Sarah's work has the uncanny ability to bewitch and infatuate. Though sceptical when I first picked up her book, being the cynical quasi-beatnik that I am, I soon lost myself to her words. And I am positive anyone who repeats my good fortune will be equally captivated.

It is a pleasure to experience these poems and an honor to be part of her book. I know you will become just as charmed as I am.

Happy reading.

~Altis Conners

Amity

We are friends
Although
We don't always agree
Although
I remind you of owed money
Although
You didn't call
Although
I forgot to write
Although
We sometimes clash

We are friends
Because
We made it through the valley
Because
We emerged on the other side
Because
We were still holding hands
Because
You were there in the dark times
Because
You were also there in the sunshine

We are friends
Just because
So my friends remember, and so Daniel won't forget

The Spell-Breaker

A black cat crossed my path today
"What rotten luck!" some would say
Maybe so, but hardly wizard's play
It was just a kitten, anyway
I picked him up, and hugged my cares away

Portrait

Gazing into the mirror
She feels ugly
And red and plain
But does not despair

She knows it's an illusion
A little makeup
The right clothes
Fixed hair— she'll look good again

She has two pretty sisters
Both younger
Both blonde
She's not overshadowed

Though she is brunette
And medium height
She has the style
Wit and humor to garner attention

She sees stealthy glances
And fancies that she
Can have any man
Any man that she really wants

Except for the one man
Who chose another
Chose another
And tainted her self-worth

So she looks into the mirror
Beauty is there
Waiting to unfold
Like the love she once planted for him

Lost, like me
Sad colony
Of tortured souls
Still this is true
Could I just find you
—In dreams of skies, or ocean's sighs—
I'd rest and sleep till I awoke
To rediscover Roanoke

They died alone
Their names unknown
No farewell kiss
Like me too
Torn from you
—I sing a song, for love that's gone—
At night, with tears, my bed I soak
Helpless to find old Roanoke

Icy rain
A bloody stain
An old, sad tale
Of death and loss
Of pain and cross
—I walk alone, my fate bemoan—
I slept until my fears awoke
Those fears of losing Roanoke

Rediscover Roanoke

Nothing's left
Of toil and sweat
No mem'ry still remains
No bloody tears
No joy or fears
—Like me too, torn from you—
My fragile heart you cruelly broke
Can we discover Roanoke?

Lost, like me
Sad colony
Of tortured souls
It died unblessed
But now finds rest
—No more goodbyes; its spirits fly—
Even though my heart you broke
Come back, and we'll find Roanoke

Vital Annoyance

Funny, the small things
that used to grate:
A new pair of shoes, a dress
she didn't need
Fine jewelry which she
never, ever wore

Clothes tossed about, dishes
left undone
Wilting plants she forgot
to water
Windows simply begging her
to wash them
Sticking her fingers in the
sauce, licking them
Razor blades she dulled
by shaving her legs.

Funny, but of all the things
that used to grate—
What he misses most and would
give his life to find again—
Are those long, blonde hairs
on his pillow

7

ALTUS, OK

They passed overhead
I saw them in flight
So graceful and sure
Like birds of the night

The planes circling the town
     around and around

We drove far away
And saw them up there
Their wings spread out wide
Controlling the air

The planes circling the town
     around and around

A base down in Altus
Where my mother once stayed
Her dad stationed there
For many long days

The planes circling the town
     around and around

Not much has since changed
Those planes are still there
Lifting and landing
Defying thin air

The planes circling the town
     around and around

For those who serve and have served our country

Fishing With Grandpa

We fished for hours that seemed to drag
I caught my hook upon a snag
He cast his line, skillful and sure
And snared a fish with its bright lure

He got a bite with his small shad
When I had none, he saw me sad
So Grandpa let me reel his in
Played that the game was mine to win

Afterwards, the sun was bright
That big sandbass put up a fight!
I struggled hard my hook to set
And tugged and dragged him to the net

We got him in, inside the boat
Within the cooler let him float
But at the end of that May day
Set him free to swim away

At long last now, it's time to go
I drive up to the docks real slow
But I'll come back some day real soon
To fish with Grandpa until noon

For Pa-Pa, and those early mornings on the lake

Cry of the Abandoned Heart

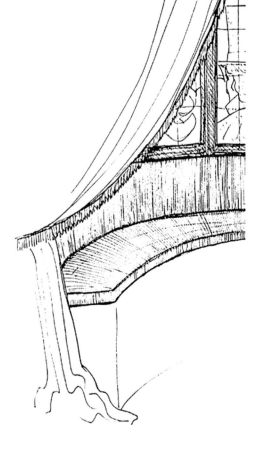

A solitary raindrop
    Trickles its reluctant way
Slowly down my window.
    I press my wrinkled palm
Flat against the glass.

Will loneliness never end?

A Strong Kind of Love

I'd bear all your burdens
    If only I could
I'd make your life happy
    Make it real good
I'll love you forever
    Both present and past
I'll be your best friend
    Through slow and through fast

Deep down where it counts
You know I'll be there
To show you I love you
Your sorrows to bear
I'll never forsake you
I won't let you go
I'll pray for you always
E'en when God tells you, "No"

I'm sorry I sometimes
Cause you to cry
I'm sorry I sometimes
Make you ask why
Just do not forsake me
We'll always be friends
I'll stick with you ever
Through thick and through thin

If ever I can
Do something for you
Please let me know
I'll cheer up your blues
This life is a journey
From start until end
But it's one I'll make with you
My sisters – my friends

In celebration of sisters everywhere,

and for Mercy and Hannah in particular

The Winter Walk

When some walk down memory's lane
What do they see?
Family, friends, home, bad or good times?
When I walk down memory's lane
I know what I see
She, him, the dogs, and me
Moonlight, starlight, blue light, and trees

We are so alike, he and I
Fearless of night
It may be cold, but it's still sweet
To be out there in the midst
Of such soft light
Blue, gentle, glowing, lovely
Like a painting, without a canvas

Those few stars glittering overhead
"Moon outshines them"
He says, and I agree with that
I mark the Little Dipper, and few else
Except that one
So bright, so blue, it outshines the rest
I'd give it a name, if one would suit

Sometimes we talk, sometimes we don't
Breezes chill me
Other than footsteps on hard earth
Toes on rocks, heels on dirt
There's them and me
And the winter silence: a melody

In summer, I walk this same path
Stays light longer
Can be out past nine, without it being
Too dark. There's snakes, though
But not in winter
I see a stick and dodge, just out of habit
You have do that sometimes, but not now

On a night like this, you expect magic
You wait to see---
Over there, by the planet Mars
"Look," we say, "a shooting star"
"What?" he asks me
And we explain, but all we get's an "Oh"
And nothing else. What more's to be said?

I step in a mud puddle
Didn't see it
Too busy watching the stars fallen into
Our pond. A night like this, even it's lovely
Do stars get wet?
I wonder that, as I stare
At the willows, the hickories, the oaks

He's so like me, cause right after I say it
"See how the moon
Shines so bright on the top of that willow tree?"
I've just pointed it out to her
So we walk on
Soon, we'll be home, where the others wait
In electric light, in mankind's domain

They didn't go; they rarely do
But that's alright
Some fear the dark, and some the night
Some fear the road: those bumps and holes
It's such a sight
The glory of tonight; I walk without fear
Admiring in the hills the lights you usually can't see

In years to come, walking memory's lane
I know what I will see
My father, my sister, our dogs and me
Strolling that dirt road, two miles in the winter
Enjoying, just being
Part of the magic of this December eve
Part of nature at its very best

In memory of those winter walks, Daddy

Dragonkind

Dragons of blue
Dragons of gold
Brilliant, wise dragons
  And dragons too bold

Dragons of black
Dragons of white
Fierce, fiery dragons
  And dragons in flight

Dragons of silver
Dragons of green
Great, horned dragons
  With scales all agleam

Dragons of war
Dragons of prey
Hoarding their treasure
  In vast, yawning caves

Dragons of myth
Dragons in tales
Little shy dragons
  With slim, forked tails

Dragons that riddle
Dragons that smile
Beware of all dragons
  Who seek to beguile

In celebration of the dragons among us.

NATURAL

Raindrops falling
Children calling
Leaves whisper
Look! He kissed her

Sunshine glowing
Green grass growing
Sparrows dart
Enraptured heart

Laughter ringing
Crickets singing
Joyful wind
Sadness ends

Mountains soaring
Oceans roaring
Stars shine
Now he's mine

Letha's Rose

<pre>
                    RED
                  ROSEBUD
               RED, RED ROSE
         SCARLET, VIVID, CRIMSON
      BLUSHING, BLEEDING, BURSTING
       BEAUTIFUL, DEEP, BRILLIANT
         ROSE PETALS, FRAGRANCE
          CRIMSON, VELVET, BOLD
            JOYFUL RED SATIN
               PETALS IN A
                 ROSEBUD
                   RED
                   RED
                   RED
                   RED
                   RED
                   RED
                   RED
                   RED
              A ROSEBUD
                ROSERED
                 PETALS
                   RED
               ROSEBED OF
                 ROSEBUD
                 PETALS
                   RED
                   RED
                   RED
                   RED
                   RED
                   RED
                   RED
                   RED
                   RED
                   RED
                   RED
                   RED
</pre>

20

A Woman's Gifts

If I could give you
Silver nights with
full moons surrounded by
hazy clouds
Yes, I would

If I could give you
And your favorite team
a National Championship
Every Year
Yes, I would

If I could give you
Autumn colors every
single day: red, yellow,
orange, and gold
Yes, I would

If I could give you
Your favorite songs
every time you turned on your
radio
Yes, I would

If I could give you
World peace
genuine happiness and
family bliss
Yes, I would

If I could give you
The story of your life
on pages of ivory with ink
of gold
Yes, I would

I can only give you
These poor gifts
my heart, my soul, my
life...myself
Will they do?

Lady

Like moonlight on satin
I shimmer
Like rosebud petals
I unfurl
Like insects on wheat
I crawl
Like newborn colts
I walk
Like pulses racing
I run
Like crimson moons
I bleed

Like grain in a field
I ripen
Like hearts aflutter
I love
Like lace on a gown
I adorn
Like emerald jade
I give life
Like raindrops falling
I nurture
Like wine in a cellar
I mature
Like snow in winter
I sleep

Life

Life is pain and love and hate
Life's a stroll through destiny's gate
Life is flight on wings that soar
Life's what makes us seek for more

Life is sunshine on a stream
Life is feeling joy's bright beam
But life is more than simply this
Life is bound up in a kiss

Life is like a baby's smile
A springtime wind, gentle and mild
Life is laughter, bliss, and thought
Life is death and dark forgot

While I live, I hold so dear
My friends and family, those most near
For life is what I know I do
When I share my heart with you

For Lydia Kurnia, FK, on FWO

Simple Pleasures

A coffee mug
A brother's hug
A horseback ride
A restless tide
A day of school
A worker's tool
A cousin's gift
A long car trip

A baby's hand
Warm golden sand
A grandpa's smile
New socks on tile
A mountain peak
A long, deep sleep
An aunt's spring flowers
A garden bower

The smell of hay
A brand-new day
A silvery moon
A whistled tune
An uncle's tease
An autumn breeze
A prosperous farm
Crocheting yarn

A child's grin
Forgiven sin
A family's love
Gifts from above

For my students, teachers, brothers, grandfathers, cousins, and family

A Mother's Heart

A mother's heart
   Is strong
   Is like no other
   Is warm

A mother's heart
   Bleeds but won't break
   Sacrifices
   Yearns for the best

A mother's heart
   Shares wisdom
   Never stops beating
   Never attacks

A mother's heart
   Never surrenders
   Is a safe place to rest
   Never gives up

A mother's heart
   Ripens with age
   And finds completeness
   In becoming

A grandmother's heart

For my own mother, grandmother, and those who've gone before

Questions

If life's a song
And time's a stream
An ever rolling, changing thing
Then who am I?
And who are you?
And what is it we're here to do?

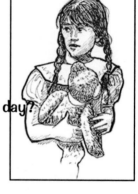

If hate is bad
And love is good
And Fate rules everything, as it should
Then shouldn't I
And shouldn't we
Be the best that we can be?

Is it the truth
What some folks say
That we should live for each new day?
And do our best,
The best we can,
To find the good in every man?

Or when we die
And drift away
Is there a place we'll always stay?
Should I worry
Or should I fear
What is there, or what is here?

Pathways to Where?

Roads commence at a single point
But soon branch out
Roads connect and intersect
Pathways to where?
Roads lead from here to everywhere
Not to Rome alone
Roads see all, know all, bear all
To the horizon
Roads can take me away or lead me home
Which road shall I choose?

CALL IT WHAT YOU WILL

Call the cat
He might not come
Call the dog
Might be the same

Call your friend
She'll pick up soon
Call your mom
She asked you to

Call the stars
By different names
Call the sun
A red-orange blaze

Call the tree
A stand of twigs
Call the sky
A bright blue bowl

Call it hate
When they don't care
Call it love
When someone does

Call it magic
When someone loves
Call it love
When magic moves

A Writer's Soul

I dream I can
Take these hands
And create something new

I dream I can
With this mind
Write fancies that ring true

I dream I can
With my pen
Steal the soul of a reader

I dream I can
With my wit
Ease the soul of the seeker

I dream I can
Take these hands
And redesign earth's look

I dream I can
Change the world
With nothing more than a book

ENSNAREMENT

Daylight blinds me

Night is my friend

...J am enslaved

These bars of iron

Embrace me fast

...in eagles talons

A prisoner of time

Forever jailed

...in this dungeon cell

J crane my neck

Trying to trace

...free footsteps above

Fantasy or reality

Does it matter

...when one is trapped?

Mercy

When Mercy brought me to that shore
I thought me home, to seek no more
When I awoke, not bound — but free
I thought it meant a changed me

Alas, she tricked me and deceived
A fool, was I, to have believed
Until I realized — slow to learn —
That Mercy did my heart discern

In my soul, she'd found scant grace
And so ignored my tear-stained face
Because I pled for only me
While all the rest forgot to see

Withholding grace, she sought to teach
That others, beyond me, I should reach
That fellow human weal and woe,
Pain and love, I ought to know

So Mercy taught me this great sooth
That hope and faith and love and truth
If used by humans, one and all
Can break down barriers, like a wall

Now upon a gleaming shore
With Mercy's aid, I've passed that door
And in the sunlight think I see
What it means to be set free

For Merty!

WHAT A BOOK CAN DO

I READ OF ANCIENT QUEENS AND KINGS
I READ OF GREEN AND GROWING THINGS

I READ OF DOCTORS FOR THE ILL
I READ OF BATTLES FOR A HILL

I READ OF LOVE, JOY, HATE, AND STRIFE
I READ THE RUDIMENTS OF LIFE

I READ OF HISTORY AND THE PAST
I READ OF SPHINXES BUILT TO LAST

I READ OF ROMANS AND THEIR LORDS
I READ OF ARMOR, SHIELDS, AND SWORDS

I READ "MY COUNTRY 'TIS OF THEE"
I READ OF FIGHTING TO BE FREE

I READ OF HAPPINESS AND WOE
I READ OF AMY, BETH, AND JO

I READ OF SLOW AND LAZY DRAWLS
I READ OF COWBOYS, GUNS, AND BRAWLS

I READ OF ROMANCE, TEARS, AND LOVE
I READ OF HEAVEN, FAR ABOVE

THE BOOKS I READ TAKE ME AWAY
WHEN I'LL RETURN, WHO CAN SAY?

Escape

I watched a ship sail on the bay
I wondered where it'd go today
Would it sail around Cape Horn
And could it be there by the morn?

I watched a ship sail on the bay
I wondered where it'd go today
Would it visit England's shore
Or knock upon old Scotland's door?

I watched a ship sail on the bay
I wondered where it'd go today
Would it find America
Or pass her by for Africa?

I watched a ship sail on the bay
I wondered where it'd go today
To Easter Island: mysterious, grim
Or to the vast, the great Stonehenge?

I watched a ship sail on the bay
I wondered where it'd go today
To Australia, where dingoes run
Or Hawaii, home of the sun?

I watched a ship sail on the bay
I wondered where it'd go today
Down to the bottom of the sea
Or to a cave, a bay, a lea?

I watched a ship sail on the bay
I wondered where it'd go today
A spot where mountains rise so high
And waterfalls drop from the sky?

I watched a ship sail on the bay
I wondered where it'd go today
Would it glide on through the night
Beneath the moon and soft starlight?

I watched a ship sail on the bay
I wondered where it'd go today
Through the fog and through the mist
To an isle that's sunshine-kissed?

I watched a ship sail on the bay
I wondered where it'd go today
Could it take me from this shore
Deposit me in days of yore?

I watched a ship sail on the bay
I wondered where it'd go today
To fetch some pearls from India's strands
Avoiding Greek and Roman bands?

I watched a ship sail on the bay
I wondered where it'd go today
Would it find something brand-new
A Viking craft, barbarian crew?

I watched a ship sail on the bay
I wondered where it'd go today
Might it find a fiend or two
A fearsome pirate and his crew?

I watched a ship sail on the bay
I wondered where it'd go today
If Spanish galleons it should see
Would it chase them 'cross the sea?

I watched a ship sail on the bay
I wondered where it'd go today
To knightly castles with towers so high
Spires that jut into the sky?

I watched a ship sail on the bay
I wondered where it'd go today
To the edges of a trail
Where cowboys ride and wagons sail?

I watched a ship sail on the bay
 I wondered where it'd go today
To regions wild and lands untamed
To realms of fantasy unnamed?

I watched a ship sail on the bay
I wondered where it'd go today
Might it spy a shy mermaid
And did it carry shells to trade?

I watched a ship sail on the bay
I wondered where it'd go today
Would it find a fairy fair
Or Elven maid with golden hair?

I watched a ship sail on the bay
I wondered where it'd go today
To a land where unicorns roam
Which sprites and pixies make their home?

I watched a ship sail on the bay
I wondered where it'd go today
To a realm of kings and queens
Of warriors bold whose weapons gleam?

I watched a ship sail on the bay
I wondered where it'd go today
To a place where dragons roar
Where winged people lift and soar?

I watched a ship sail on the bay
I wished it might take me away
I cannot go this time, I fear
But there's always another year!

For those who dream of escape...

Slave's Song

THE ETERNAL CITY
FROM SEVEN HILLS SPRINGS
THE SUN ON WHITE MARBLE
TOO BRIGHTLY DOTH GLEAM

MY HANDS ARE BOUND BACK
MY FEET TREAD ALONG
IN THE DEPTHS OF MY MIND
I CHANT A SLAVE'S SONG

A SONG OF LAMENT
A SONG MEANT TO MOURN
THE DEATH AND DESTRUCTION
OF THAT MONSTROUS MORN

ROME CAME IN THE NIGHT
AND ATTACKED IN THE DAY
ITS LEGIONS OF SWORDS
CARVING THE WAY

ONE GAVE THE COMMAND---
HIS SOLDIERS DID SLAUGHTER
THOUGH THEY SLEW THE FATHER
HE SPARED THE DAUGHTER

HE'S SAID ME NO WORDS
BUT LENT ME HIS HAND
AND ENSURED I PREVAILED
WHEN CROSSING HOT SANDS

45

WE ENTER HIS CITY
THE SOLDIER, THE SLAVE
FOR HIM, ALL THE TRIUMPH
FOR ME, NAUGHT BUT CHAINS

SO LOWLY AM I
BUT WHAT DO I SEE?
HIS HEAD TURNS TO LOOK--
DARK EYES FALL ON ME

THEY'LL TAKE ME TO SLAVERS
WHO CARE NOT TO WOO
SHOULD THE TRIBUNE COME PURCHASE ME
PRAY, WHAT WILL I DO?

For Jill, who shares my love of history and Ben Hur.

𝔙iking

MISTS DIVIDE AND TIMBERS CREAK
    THE SKIES RELEASE COLD SNOW AND SLEET

BLACK SHIPS SAIL AND RAVENS FLY
    THEY'LL BE HERE SOON, NOT BY AND BY

A DRAGON HEAD AND MYRIAD OARS
    LO! THEY ALIGHT UPON YON SHORE

ARMOR, FUR, AND SWORD, AND SPEAR
    THE COMING RAID DRAWS NEAR, DRAWS NEAR

MARCHING BOOTS AND TRAMPLING FEET
    SCOUTS SPRINT AHEAD - DARK, SWIFT AND SLEEK

POWERS OLD AND MAGIC WILD
    I FREEZE IN FEAR, A FRIGHTENED CHILD

Raid

A FEW MEN FIGHT WITH SHIELD AND SPEAR
 THEY'RE CUT DOWN SWIFTLY, LIKE A DEER

BLADES ARE DAMP WITH BLOOD AND GORE
 THE RAIDERS STEAL, COME BACK FOR MORE

FIRES BURN AND CHILDREN WEEP
 THE NORSEMEN LEAVE, O'ER PATHS SO STEEP

MISTS DIVIDE AND TIMBERS CREAK
 AS FROM MY HIDING PLACE I SNEAK

OARS LIFT AND FALL TO RISE AGAIN
 I CREEP BACK HOME TO FACE THEIR SIN

SUNSHINE DEPARTS AND FADES AWAY
 WHEN THEY'LL RETURN, NONE CAN SAY

For Carol, who tolerates and shares my idiosyncrasies…

Pirate's Prize

The sea claimed me
But I escaped
Only to fall prey to
Pirate hands

The captain claimed me
Different, he
His share of the prize
That was me

The captain claimed me
But set me free
Liberty claimed me
And I ran

Now, I drift across
Golden sands
I escaped but-
Did my heart?

Dance of War

Blades of steel reflect the light
As they move from left to right
We are the ones, the chosen few
We dance the dance of war anew

Over and under, up and down
See us move, to victory bound
We are the ones, the chosen few
We dance the dance of war anew

Our hearts pound madly in our chests
As we strive to know who's best
We are the ones, the chosen few
We dance the dance of war anew

Taking the Dead

It happened like this
It happened this way
Finding a plantation
He decided to stay

The house was in ruins
The stables no more
The owners were gone
He knelt on the floor—

To build him a fire
But felt a strange chill
Bidding him glance up
(He started and thrilled)

To glimpse a young girl
Of ten and of nine
Dressed up in wide hoopskirts
And flounces so fine

For only an instant
This vision was seen
The flick of an eyelid
Oh, was it a dream?

He leapt up and chased her
But nothing was found
He called and he searched
The house and its grounds

Still nothing, so with
An eerie, sad heart
He went back inside
To fire and hearth

But that night he dreamed
He saw her again
He woke to her weeping—
Or was it the wind?

His sleep was disturbed
He could not forget
The frail southern elf
Whom briefly he'd met

The house full of shadows
Of death and of rot
Of sorrows of people
His own folk had shot

Next morning at dawn
The sky was all gold
He searched near and far
And found her dead, cold

Her family all murdered
Herself taken too
Her plantation ransacked
By deserters in blue

What curse was upon her
What terrible fear
Had bade her ghost linger
Haunting him here?

But seeing her lie there
So small and so still
He knew that he loved her

With all of his will

Though he was a Yankee
And she a grey elf
He lay down beside her
Gathered her to himself

His grandmother's ring
From his pocket he stole
And placed on her finger
Offering his soul

His ring on her hand
One last kiss, one touch
He's taking her with him
He loves her that much

In days yet to come
They will not be found
They both will be gone
High Heavenward bound

"The living take their dead with them when they die."
-Tillie Olsen, *Tell Me a Riddle*

The Magic of Midnight

The Magic of Midnight
Through stardrops it streams
Like swathes of black velvet
Like diamonds on rings

While filling my soul
It's taking me there
Far, far from this earth
And into frail air

The Magic of Midnight
Or is it a curse?
It's snatching my mind—
To heal or make worse?

Those stars on deep velvet
Those galaxies of ice-blue
Cartwheeling and tumbling
Re-birth me anew

I'm changing, I'm altered
By enchantments so fine
By ghosts of the night
By moonlight sublime

Yet, once I return
What then shall I be?
A bright, celestial being
Or still mortal me?

Sharp swords they are cutting
My flesh they do tear
No rusty or dull blades
To sliver me here

The Magic of Midnight
No longer myself—
I light upon earth
To dwell as an Elf

For Rusty

sun slayer

Wings of darkness fill the sky
Blotting stars that float so high
And I think, I dream, I see
A face that smiles, smiles at me

Young I was at ten and four
When I found that secret door
And there it was I thought I saw
A horrid beast with slavering maw

It took me down, so deep and low
Through loamy soil and blowing snow
And when I woke it was to see
The king of green life watching me

He taught me secrets, traded there
All he knew for long blonde hair
Mine it was he took, and stole
Sunlight bright…along with my soul.

Green life needs sun, the sun and rain
To make new plants live again
And I, he used to steal the sun
I lost it all. He won, he won

He let me go, but not too far
Alas, I'm lonely like a star
I laid alone on grass of green
'Neath silent stars I'd never seen

The sun was gone and in its place
A horde of stars I could not trace
The sun was gone, and what was I
But Slayer to lord of the sky?

I made a deal and shook her hand
Dove deep beneath the desert sands
Where heat from sun still existed
We took the heat and fetched and lifted

She bore it on her wings so fine
I tied it with gold hair of mine
We two, the fairy queen and I
Rebirthed the sun into the sky

He knew our trick and grew quite mad
He killed the queen and made me sad
I mourned the fairy's loss of life
Cut short with evil, magic knife

He took me too but I resisted
Caught his face, restrained and kissed it
He forgot anger, forwent wrath
Released me on my homeward path

Two years later he returned
Seasons had changed and much he'd learned
Of life and love and stars and sun
And what we want, we will become

He loved me, took me as his wife
Blonde peasant girl—king of green life
Deep in the bowels of the earth
In bejeweled caves did I give birth

Happy was I but longed to see
Just one more time land, sun, and sea
He caught me up in arms so strong
Flew me away on journey long

There he left me in the grass
On my back I felt the hours pass
He soon came back but I resisted
"A little longer," I insisted

He gave till night, king of green life
Then come I must, no fight or strife
To palace-caves and caverns deep
To chambers of rocks wherein we sleep

He then arrived on wings he'd stole
Fairy wings of blue and gold
To fetch me back, his bride and wife
Slayer of the Sun, king of green life

Lo I see him, see him come
Night veils the sky and moon the sun
His borrowed wings, so strong they beat
Stir grass and flowers 'round my feet.

He stoops and lifts me, gently there
Brown-skinned fingers tangle hair
Kissing me, he bids me fly
Through miles and miles of nighttime sky

We're going home now, it is time
Wings bear us swift through starlit sky
Glancing up, I dream I see
A smile for Sun Slayer . . . lowly me

BINDING CURSE

I cut the night and make it bleed
To show the world my pain, my need
I blot the stars from yonder sky
You ask me why, ask who am I?

You tell me life is not forlorn
With each new dawn, man is reborn
But I tell you, tell you true
For some of us, there's nothing new

I've lived forever in this shell
Heard ghosts of death tell such sad tales
Seen battles waged and lost and won
Seen moons fall down, give way to sun

I craved dark magic, though I knew
For mercy afterwards, I'd sue
For mercy, peace, forgiveness, love—
For gifts of healing, from above

And now I'm doomed in night to roam
Lost in hate, barred from my home
If you see me, best take care
And of my sinful past, beware

Though I am great, I am alone
For me, the power of a throne
Is naught compared with sweet, fresh air
And wholesome love that others share

Power's a curse, and want is blind
Sin's a grip that ever binds
So to my warning give you heed
Into dark magic, let none you lead

For Asi, on FWO

The Dreamer

On shores of gold she moves her feet
To say she walks down yonder street
---would be a lie

On fields of green she yearns to lay
And sing ethereal hours away
---in a lullaby

She is a Dreamer, bright and fair
Watch her, catch her, if you dare
---to break your heart

For Dreamers dance while other weep
And live their lives while others sleep
---in nighttimes art

DRAGON CALL

The horned dragon came
　　　While the maid sang
Her song to an evening breeze

With wings of bright red
　　　It hovered o'erhead
And laughed when she tried to flee

His teeth gleaming white
　　　His claws black as night
He growled and followed the maid

"Come, come, did not you
　　　Expect me to view
When you sang out this call for my aid?"

Halted in flight
　　　She swallowed her fright
And decided she must be brave

"Good dragon," said she
　　　"It isn't mere me
"But my love that I ask you to save"

"Well, tell me of him"
　　　Urged the beast with a grin
And so she related her tale

A witch bent on sin
　　　Had taken, changed him
Into a dragon with wing, fang, and scale

"Knowing one dragon song
　　"And it, being long
"I sang it aloud, just hoping he'd hear"

"Perhaps he has heard?"
　　Hoping it not too absurd
She asked the fierce beast so near

　"Oh please have no fear
　　"And shed no more tears
"For your song, it has done the trick"

And before her two eyes
　　The beast diminished in size---
Her magic song had outwitted the witch

So, happily together
　　With marriage their tether
Maiden and man shared their laughter

No more dragon form
　　No more sad hearts torn
They lived happily ever after

For Lydia M...

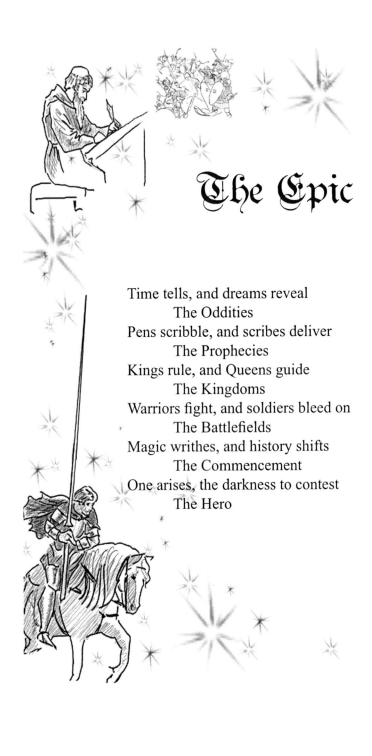

The Epic

Time tells, and dreams reveal
    The Oddities
Pens scribble, and scribes deliver
    The Prophecies
Kings rule, and Queens guide
    The Kingdoms
Warriors fight, and soldiers bleed on
    The Battlefields
Magic writhes, and history shifts
    The Commencement
One arises, the darkness to contest
    The Hero

A man strives, whom a woman adores
   The Romance
Shadows deepen, the Light contests
   The Battleground
Sacrifices are offered, and evil crushed
   The Victory
A woman weeps, a warrior finds rest
   The Outcome
Honors earned, love slowly heals
   The Continuance
Stars spin and peace reigns
   The End

This one, TommyG, is for you, with my thanks

Homeschooled by her parents along with her five siblings, Sarah Ashwood graduated her family's home high school in May 2003. She is now a full-time college student working towards a B.A. in English with an emphasis on creative writing. She is a member of the International Honor Society, Phi Theta Kappa, and has been selected for the National Dean's List. Sarah has recently joined a second honour society, The Golden Key.

Sarah's poetry was first published in the October 2007 edition of *Art and Prose*. In November of 2007 she won first place in a local literary contest for an essay on the importance of reading. Since that time, her work—both poetry and prose, fiction and non-fiction—has appeared in such publications as *Aoife's Kiss*, *Flashing Swords Press*, *Mindflights*, *Outdoors Spectacular*, *The Lorelei Signal*, *Abandoned Towers*, *New Myths,* and *TeenAge*. Future work will appear in *Silver Blade*, *Homeschooling Today*, and *Devozine*. Sarah and her cousin Carol Green are also co-editors of the fantasy ezine, *Moon Drenched Fables*.

Along with school, Sarah is always hard at work on her writing. For her Young Adult fantasy novel, *Knight's Rebirth*, she is under currently contract with Cyberwizard Productions. Besides this, she has completed a fantasy trilogy and a work of inspirational fiction. Five additional novels are also in the works, with plenty more planned for the future! In her spare time, Sarah enjoys fitness, hand quilting, reading, playing the piano, traveling, attending the opera and ballet with friends, and homeschooling her two young students, Hunter and Zachary, along with her sisters, Mercy and Hannah.

For more information, visit her website at www. sarahashwood.homestead.com

Printed in the United States
143055LV00001B/3/P